Pets

Activities for 3–5 Year Olds

Sue Pearce and
Caroline Quin

Brilliant
PUBLICATIONS

We hope you enjoy using this book. If you would like further information on other titles published by Brilliant Publications, please write to the address given below or look on our website: www.brilliantpublications.co.uk.

Other books in the Activities for 3–5 Year Olds series:

All About Us
Caring and Sharing
Colours
Families
Food

Gardening
Shopping
Water
Weather

Published by Brilliant Publications,
Unit 10, Sparrow Hall Farm, Edlesborough, Bedfordshire, LU6 2ES
website: www.brilliantpublications.co.uk

Written by Sue Pearce and Caroline Quin
Second edition revised and updated in 2012 by Debbie Chalmers
Illustrated by Claire Boyce

© Sue Pearce and Caroline Quin
Printed ISBN 978 0 85747 665 4
ebook ISBN 978 0 85747 092 8

The Publisher accepts no responsibility for accidents arising from the activities described in this book.

First published in 1998, reprinted 2012, second edition 2012
10 9 8 7 6 5 4 3 2 1

Contents

	Page
Introduction	4

Communication and language

Which pet is yours?	6
Pet stories	8
Who am I?	10

Physical development

Pets' needs	12
Rubbings of our pets	14
Pretending to be a…	16

Personal, social and emotional development

Who has a pet?	18
Who will mind the pet?	20
Goldfish collage	22

Literacy

My grandma's cat	24
Rhymes, rhymes, rhymes	26

Mathematics

Matching pets	28
Tortoise drive	30
Sizing them up or down	32

	Page

Understanding the world

Mix or match	34
Spot the difference	36
A pet with a difference	38
Working pets	40
Snailarium	42
What gerbils eat	44
Tropical fish mobiles	46
Creepy crawly lotto	48

Expressive arts and design

I went for a walk one morning	50
I can paint a…	52
Snail trail	54
Sounds like our pets	56
Aunty Flo had a…	58
Making a snail	60

To avoid the clumsy 'he/she', the child is referred to throughout as 'she'.

Introduction

Keeping small pet animals in an early years setting can be of benefit to all the children, but particularly those who are unable to keep pets at home. Children can experience:

* learning to respect and care for living and growing things
* exploring and recognizing features of animals
* learning about different creatures' needs for food, water and specific types of habitat.

The activities in this book are linked to the Early Learning Goals of the Department for Education's revised *Statutory Framework for the Early Years Foundation Stage* (September 2012), and its guidance document, *Development Matters*. They recognize that children learn through playing and exploring, creating and thinking critically.

The role of an early years practitioner is to provide stimulating and challenging activities within an enabling environment. Ideas must be flexible enough to meet the needs of each individual as a unique child and to build upon the children's knowledge and interests to promote active learning. All of the activities in this book may be easily adapted to suit individual children or groups of any size.

When keeping pets, you will need to make sure that:
* there is a member of staff personally responsible for the welfare of the animals
* you can provide a suitable environment (for

advice see RSPCA website: www.rspca.org.uk/
allaboutanimals/pets)
* you can provide suitable housing, food, drink,
  cleansing and veterinary care at all times, including
  weekends and holidays
* you can afford to keep the animals and meet any
  veterinary fees
* contact between animals and children is supervised
  and controlled at all times
* the animals get adequate rest, away from
  disturbance
* the animals are prevented from indiscriminate
  breeding
* the animals will not pose health and safety
  problems such as animal-borne diseases, allergies
  or injury to the children
* you comply with current legislation.

When it is not possible to keep small pet animals in
a setting, other ways of providing the children with
opportunities to observe animals could be to:
* observe animals in the outdoor area or a nearby
  park or field
* encourage small wild animals into the garden by
  providing appropriate habitats
* hunt for mini-beasts to study, being careful not to
  disturb or destroy their habitats
* arrange with neighbours who own pets (such as
  cats, rabbits or guinea pigs) that the children may
  make regular or occasional visits to stroke and play
  with them, and watch or help while they are being
  fed or groomed
* use DVDs, pictures, CD-ROMs, posters and models
  of the animals.

Which pet is yours?

Learning opportunities
* Participating in a discussion about pets, listening and responding to others and speaking confidently within a familiar group

Links to the Early Learning Goals
* Communication and language – Listening and attention, Speaking

Also
* Literacy – Reading

Equipment and resources
Photographs of children's own pets (where possible); pictures of pets from magazines, posters, etc; word cards, printed clearly in lower case: 'cat', 'dog', etc.

Activity
Working in small groups ask the children to show pictures of their own pets and talk about them. Offer support and encouragement by asking their pets' names and colours and what they like to eat. A child who does not have a pet may choose a picture of one, describe it, make up a name and guess what it would like to eat. Suggest that the children ask each other questions about their own pets, those of friends and relations, or pets they would like to have.

Extension

Encourage children to sort the magazine pictures into groups of pets (dogs, cats, etc) and to keep them in trays or envelopes or to stick them onto paper as collages. Ask them to read the word cards, sounding them out phonetically if necessary, to label the different animals in the pictures.

Discussion

Ask whether any of the children's families, or any people they know, have an unusual pet, such as a snake or a lizard.

Pet stories

Learning opportunities
* Listening to a story with attention and concentration and responding to what is heard

Links to the Early Learning Goals
* Communication and language – Listening and attention

Also
* Expressive arts and design – Being imaginative

Equipment and resources
No special equipment.

Activity
Storytelling without books is an important skill as it allows the teller to adjust the story to suit the situation. Discuss the basic plot of the story with the children before beginning to tell it to the group. Find out if they have any pets or would like to own one.

Tell a story about a pet. Perhaps it is a surprise pet that a child has been longing for. Perhaps it is an expected pet, like a baby kitten, which is not ready to leave its mother yet. Perhaps it is a pet belonging to someone else and the child is asked to look after it. Bring the children into the story by name, eg 'Gemma was going to see a kitten that she would be able to bring home when it was old enough.' Miss out words, or hesitate occasionally, to encourage the children to join in.

Extension

Ask questions about the story to check the children's understanding. If appropriate, produce props such as a collar and lead, a brush, or a pet toy. Talk about the grooming of pets.

Discussion

Encourage the children to contribute ideas to the story by inviting them to choose names for pets and to answer questions about their needs.

Who am I?

Learning opportunities
* Listening and concentration skills
* Using experience and imagination to identify animals from verbal descriptions and clues

Links to the Early Learning Goals
* Communication and language – Listening and attention

Also

* Understanding the world – The world

Equipment and resources
A4 size picture cards of six to eight pet animals (as life size as possible for small animals); prepared descriptions or clues of each pet, broken down into small sections (don't make them too obvious).

Activity
Sit in a small group with a maximum of three or four children. Hold the cards so that the children can't see the pictures. Tell them you are going to describe one of the pets, giving clues. The child who guesses correctly takes that picture. If a few children work out the answers more quickly every time than the rest of the group, ask individual children in turn instead, so that they all have a chance to answer.

Extension

At the end of the game, sort the pictures into sizes or types, etc. Talk about the baby pet animals' names, the differences between one newborn pet animal and another newborn. Knowledge of length of pregnancies might be useful!

Discussion

Discuss how some animals in the wild are distantly related to our pet animals. Ask whether the children can think of some, such as lions and tigers/cats and wolves/dogs.

Pets' needs

Learning opportunities
* Developing an understanding of healthy and suitable diets for people and animals, and their similarities and differences, and the time, equipment and skills needed to care for a pet

Links to the Early Learning Goals
* Physical development – Health and self-care
Also
* Understanding the world – The world

Equipment and resources
Pictures or silhouettes of pet animals (you could use the ones made for Matching pets, page 28) mounted on A4 card (one per card); smaller pictures of equipment and food which are generally provided for/required by each type of pet animal (also mounted on card).

Activity
Work with a small group of children. Give them two or three pictures or silhouettes and a pile of assorted equipment and food pictures. Support the children as they sort these and decide which foods and pieces of equipment belong with each animal picture or silhouette. Now include pictures of people and their foods and decide which foods are for people only, which are for animals only and which can be eaten by either. Further divide the food for people by deciding which of their foods are healthy and which are better when eaten only occasionally.

Extension

Talk about the suitability of 'swapping' equipment and foods and how the people and the pet animals would manage (or not). Have some examples of some of the pet food/equipment for the children to see and handle where appropriate.

Discussion

Talk about the types of food that each type of animal eats and how many different foods some of them eat compared with others. Compare people's and animals' types and variety of foods. Emphasize the importance of a healthy diet for all living creatures.

Rubbings of our pets

Learning opportunities
* Developing and improving hand/eye coordination
  and small movement control
* Handling tools and equipment effectively

Links to the Early Learning Goals
* Physical development – Moving and handling

Equipment and resources
Templates of pets (available from various educational
suppliers, or make your own from card); white A4
paper; thick crayons (with paper removed); sharp
pencils.

Activity
Demonstrate for children how to hold the paper over
the template with one hand and the crayon flat in
the other. Model rubbing the crayon across the paper
to create an impression of the template underneath.
(This activity requires considerable small muscle
control and manual dexterity, as it is difficult to hold
the paper still while pressing hard enough with the
moving crayon. Support some children if necessary,
by helping to hold the paper still at times and
modelling the arm movement again.)

Extension

Using very sharp pencils, demonstrate how to draw around the templates on top of the paper and encourage children to copy and join in. Model how to hold the template still with one hand and draw with the pencil in the other, lifting a hand to draw underneath as necessary. Again, some children may need support to hold the template still or to coordinate the movements of their pencils.

Discussion

Reassure the children of how difficult it is for anyone to hold the template and the crayon at the same time. Praise their successes and achievements and offer help and support to prevent frustration that would spoil the activity.

Pretending to be a...

Learning opportunities
* Developing balance, coordination and control of large and small movements
* Exploring animal role-play

Links to the Early Learning Goals
* Physical development – Moving and handling
Also
* Expressive arts and design – Being imaginative

Equipment and resources
Large clear area; some large apparatus, to include: a wooden ladder and safety mats, crash/floor mats, free-standing hoops, tunnels, balls, etc.

Activity
Help the children to form small groups and ask them to stay within these groups and work in different areas, for safety. The children may pretend to be the appropriate animals while moving in each of the areas. Ask the groups to move on at intervals until everyone has had a turn at working in each area. For example, you might have:

* hamsters — tunnel
* fish or snakes — slithering on floor mats
* budgies — climbing up/down the ladder
* cats — playing with a ball
* dogs — jumping through hoops

Divide the children into groups. At each area the children pretend to be that animal and move in the appropriate way. Rotate the groups between areas.

Extension

Encourage the children to make the noise and/or behave like the relevant pet when at the activity area.

Discussion

Encourage the children to describe what it felt like to pretend to be the pets and to move like them and make their noises. Ask which of the pets they would most like to be and encourage them to say why.

Who has a pet?

Learning opportunities
* Understanding and respecting that people have different needs, wishes and opinions and discussing these cooperatively and sensitively within a familiar group

Links to the Early Learning Goals
* Personal, social and emotional development – Making relationships

Also
* Understanding the world – People and communities

Equipment and resources
Some pictures of pets.

Activity
Look at the pet pictures with the children and encourage them to chat with each other about their own pets and to talk freely about their feelings regarding other pets they know or the ones in the pictures.

Talk to the children about who has, and who does not have, a pet. Talk about the reasons why people keep pets. Ask why some people cannot have a pet: maybe someone in the family is allergic to animal fur; perhaps they live in a flat which would be unsuitable for pets; perhaps most of the family are out all day so the pet would get very lonely; perhaps the food for the pet would cost too much money.

Extension

Ask the children whether they help to care for pets
at home or in relatives' or friends' houses. Think
together of the types of tasks that are needed, such
as feeding the cat, cleaning out the rabbit hutch and
taking the dog for a walk, and talk about who at home
usually carries out most of the tasks.

Discussion

Since this is a discussion activity the talk can go in
many directions and the children should be allowed
as much freedom as possible to explore and verbalize
their knowledge, ideas and feelings about pets. Talk
also about why some people find comfort from their
pets. Perhaps they are all alone and their pet is their
best friend. Perhaps they like stroking their pet and
the pet is always nice to them.

Who will mind the pet?

Learning opportunities

* Understanding the need to treat pets with care and respect and to be concerned for their happiness and well-being
* Remembering responsibilities and the need to take turns and share out tasks and commitments

Links to the Early Learning Goals

* Personal, social and emotional development – Managing feelings and behaviour, Making relationships

Equipment and resources

A large piece of paper or card; some felt-tipped pens; a prepared list of dates; a list of jobs; a list of the children's names.

Activity

Working with a small group of children, draw up a list of tasks for the care of any pets in the setting. For example, buying food, feeding, cleaning out, grooming, taking them home at weekends and taking them home over holidays. Make a rota chart with the advice, suggestions and help of the children. Ensure that only children who have permission from their parents are assigned to take the pet home. Children who do not have this permission may be allocated other care tasks within the setting.

Extension

Share the chart with the whole group and discuss what each section means. Write the children's names onto cards that can be attached to the chart (using magnetic strips, velcro, blu-tack, etc) alongside days of the week and the dates of weekends and holidays, to show whose job it is to take care of the pets. Share the task of changing the name of the person responsible for the pets with everyone at a group or circle time each day. More than one child may take her turn at the same time, especially if there is more than one pet, and two or more names may be selected for some or all of the tasks.

Discussion

Talk about the importance of proper care. Ask the children what would happen if the pets were not cared for properly. Show that a pet is a responsibility as well as a friend. Help the children to find out how 'relatives' of their pets, such as rabbits or fish, look after themselves in the wild.

Goldfish collage

Learning opportunities
* Approaching a new craft activity with confidence and discussing it within a familiar group
* Speaking from experience, expressing likes and dislikes and selecting resources and techniques independently in collage work

Links to the Early Learning Goals
* Personal, social and emotional development – Self-confidence and self-awareness

Also

* Expressive arts and design – Exploring and using media and materials, Being imaginative

Equipment and resources
Goldfish shapes of different sizes, cut out of stiff paper or card; lots of different shiny and bright pieces to stick onto the fish, such as orange, yellow, red and gold paper, card, tissue paper, crêpe paper, cellophane, felt, fabric scraps, sequins, stickers, ribbons and buttons; PVA glue; spreaders; containers for the glue and for the collage items.

Activity
If possible, look at real goldfish or pictures of them in books before introducing the activity. Discuss the fish with the children and encourage them to offer ideas for making their collages. Describe the various materials that will be available and invite them to say which they like best and whether there are any that they don't want to use and why.

Tell them that they may make as many fish as they like, in any sizes they choose.

Support children in sharing resources and using techniques, to prevent frustration that would otherwise spoil a child's enjoyment and achievement, but allow each child to concentrate on her own craft project and to complete it in her own way. She may make a collage that is hardly recognizable as a goldfish or one that looks very realistic. Ask children if they would like to tell you about their fish after the activity ends.

Extension
Suspend different-sized fish in boxes on black thread to make your own aquarium. Invite the children to paint the inside and the outside of the boxes to their own designs.

Discussion
Talk about where goldfish live (eg in ponds, in tanks and in bowls). Ask the children to think about the goldfish and pictures of goldfish that they have seen and to say whether they are actually all 'gold' or orange-coloured. (Some have patches on them and some are almost white.) Ask if anyone has seen golden carp, which look like huge goldfish.

My grandma's cat

Learning opportunities
* Reading repeating words in sentences
* Using adjectives to describe cats and other animals

Links to the Early Learning Goals
* Literacy – Reading

Also

* Communication and language – Understanding, Speaking

Equipment and resources
Word cards, printed clearly in lower case, to make up the six repeating words of the sentence; blank cards; black pen.

Activity
Spread the word cards out and arrange them in order, so that they make the sentence: 'My grandma's cat is a ... cat.' Read the sentence with the children, following the words from left to right with a finger as they are said. Invite the children to suggest words to describe the cat. Write the words onto blank cards and put them, one by one, into the correct place in the sentence, reading the whole sentence with the children each time. You could vary the activity by asking the children to suggest more exotic pets that their grandma might own. Ask the children to suggest words to describe those animals.

Extension

As the children get more confident the game can be played using the alphabet. For example: 'My grandma's cat is an **attractive** cat'; 'My grandma's cat is a **beautiful** cat', and so on.

Discussion

Experiment with words and decide whether all the words that have been used to describe a cat could describe another animal, such as a camel. Ask children whether they have grandmothers and whether they really do have pets. Talk about some older people having pets for companionship.

Rhymes, rhymes, rhymes

Learning opportunities
* Experimenting with words and rhymes
* Creating rhyming sentences, writing them down and reading them aloud

Links to the Early Learning Goals
* Literacy – Reading, Writing
Also
* Communication and language - Speaking

Equipment and resources
List of types of pets: eg cat, kitten, dog, puppy; list of pets' names or potential names: eg Spot, Rover, Felix, Lucky, Snowball, Tinker.

Activity
Give the children an example of a rhyme, eg cat/fat. Invite them to try to make up similar rhymes. Ask them to try to rhyme the names of their pets with another word, eg Lucky/mucky. Extend the activity by making up more lengthy rhymes, such as 'The fat cat sat on the mat', with the help of the children. If the children can't think of a real word that rhymes, they could make one up.

They could write down the word, then change the first letter and read the word aloud again, several times, until they see or hear a rhyme that would make sense.

Extension

Find suitable pictures and write the rhymes under them. Display the pictures.

Discussion

(Be prepared for rude words to occur at times, as swift rhyming often leads to this, but encourage children immediately to find alternatives.) Introduce the children to the phrase: 'You're a poet and you didn't know it.' Challenge them to find rhymes for more unusual pets, such as stick insects.

Matching pets

Learning opportunities
* Developing shape recognition
* Matching and sorting skills

Links to the Early Learning Goals
* Mathematics – Shape, space and measures

Equipment and resources
Pictures of various pets, black paper, white or coloured card, scissors, glue, laminator.

Activity
Draw or cut out pictures of different pets, then trace their outlines exactly onto black paper and cut them out as silhouettes. Stick both the pictures and the silhouettes separately onto pieces of card. Laminate the cards.

Work with a small group of children. Spread the complete pictures on the table. Hold the silhouettes and deal them out to the children, one each. Ask the children to match their silhouette to the appropriate picture. As the children become more proficient, make new cards where the differences between the pets are less obvious. For example, you could have two rabbits, one with both ears sticking straight up, the other with one ear up and the other folded down. Encourage the children to concentrate on the details and spot the small differences. Suggest that they help each other when they are stuck or unsure.

Extension
Leave the game out on the table and allow the
children to play with it by themselves.

Discussion
Talk about how the shapes match and where the
similarities and differences lie. Suggest clues that they
might look for.

Tortoise drive

Learning opportunities
* Recognizing numbers one to six
* Counting skills
* Playing cooperatively within a small group
* Understanding and following the rules of a simple game, with adult support if needed

Links to the Early Learning Goals
* Mathematics – Numbers

Also
* Personal, social and emotional development – Making relationships
* Communication and language - Understanding

Equipment and resources
A5 piece of card per player, black pen, number die, laminator, six large counters per player, (also 21 small counters per player and small bowls to keep counters in – optional).

Activity
Prepare one tortoise game card per player by drawing a picture similar to the illustration shown and tracing it onto as many A5 pieces of card as required, then laminating the cards.

Work with groups of four to six children (use a smaller group size with younger children and only large counters). To play the game with the group: Each player has a tortoise card and a bowl of counters. The first player throws the die. The player finds the number thrown on his card and covers it using a large counter. Players take turns to throw the die until all the numbered parts of the tortoise have been covered. If a player throws a number he has already covered, then he passes the die on to the next player.

Extension

This game can be extended by using the small counters. Instead of covering the number with a large counter, the child places the corresponding number of small counters on the table beside the tortoise card.

Discussion

Talk about tortoises as pets and whether any of the children have one or know anyone who does. If so, try to arrange for it to visit the setting. It is a fascinating but very safe animal for children to observe. Anyone with experience of a tortoise can talk about what it looks like, what it feels like when touched, what it eats, how it moves and whether it is always slow. Also introduce the subject of hibernation and how tortoises may bury themselves in the garden or be put safely into boxes in sheds for the winter by their owners.

Sizing them up or down

Learning opportunities
* Understanding gradual increases and reductions in size
* Sorting and matching skills

Links to the Early Learning Goals
* Mathematics – Shape, space and measures
Also
* Understanding the world – Technology

Equipment and resources
Paper, stiff card, photocopier, scissors, laminator.

Prepare the cards for the activity first. On a sheet of paper make simple drawings of four to six pet animals (eg gerbil, cat, dog, guinea pig, fish, parakeet). They should be no more than 7 cm x 7 cm each. Photocopy the sheet once in this size, then photocopy it again four or five times more, remembering each time to gradually reduce the size of the photocopy. Cut the pictures out and mount them onto pieces of stiff card. Each card must be the same size – approximately 9 cm x 9 cm. Laminate all the cards. You should end up with five (or more) cards of each pet animal whose size gradually ranges from 7 cm x 7 cm down to about 2 cm x 2 cm.

Allow children to watch the photocopier and the laminator as you use them, and, under careful supervision, to press a button or take out a sheet of

paper or finished copy from the tray. Describe what
the machines are doing as they work.

Activity

Put all the cards into a pile and invite children
to match the same animals and sort them into
'pet families', then to sort each family again into
graduating sizes.

Extension

Children could re-sort cards into same size pet
groups.

Discussion

Talk about how things can be of the same type, but
very different in size. Look around the room and see
what is the same type but of different size, eg tables,
chairs, windows, children, adults, books, etc.

Mix or match

Learning opportunities
* Understanding the characteristics of particular pet animals and the differences between them
* Using both experience and imagination to think about what might happen if parts of the animals were swapped or combined

Links to the Early Learning Goals
* Understanding the world – The world

Also

* Expressive arts and design – Being imaginative

Equipment and resources
Bold outline drawings of common pets divided into four sections: head, body, legs, tail (draw the lines on the sheet first, then add the details to fit – try to make the parts from the different animals interchangeable by drawing them in approximately the same sizes and positions and away from the dividing lines); photocopier with white paper; four shallow trays (optional); PVA glue; brushes or spreaders; black or dark paper.

Activity
Photocopy several copies of the pet outlines. Cut out the pieces and sort them according to type of body part. Put each part into a separate shallow tray or pile. Invite the children to choose one piece from each tray or pile (head, body, legs and tail) and to stick them together on a sheet of dark paper to create a 'new' pet.

Alternatively, they could try to find and match the sections that re-form one of the pets correctly.

Extension

Talk about how you could take parts or features of one thing and combine them with parts or features of something else, in order to create something new or more useful.

Discussion

Think and talk with the children about how animals would look if some of their body parts were swapped, eg a budgie with an elephant's nose. Ask the children what problems they think the new-look birds and animals could encounter.

Spot the difference

Learning opportunities
* Looking carefully at similar pictures and noticing small differences
* Purposeful mark making

Links to the Early Learning Goals
* Understanding the world – The world
Also
* Physical development – Moving and handling

Equipment and resources
Paper; pencil; stiff card; photocopier; correcting fluid; laminator; scissors; water-based marker pens.

Activity
Make a line drawing of a pet on a sheet of paper, or find a suitable animal outline, and make two photocopies of it.

Photocopy this picture again, so that the alterations are not obvious. Mount the drawings side by side onto card and laminate the page.

Repeat the same process with other types of pets.

Invite children to choose cards and pens and to look for differences and mark the ones they spot, by drawing a circle around them or by drawing the missing pieces. (Wipe the cards clean with a damp cloth afterwards, to remove the extra marks and make them ready for other children to use.)

Extension

The cards could be made more complex by using
more detailed drawings or by increasing the number
of details which the child has to find. The size of the
cards may need to be increased.

Discussion

Look for and talk about similarities and differences
between objects in the room. Ask children to tell the
group about the differences they have spotted.

A pet with a difference

Learning opportunities

* Understanding that farm animals can also be pets and that living in different areas and environments can make different types of pet more appropriate

Links to the Early Learning Goals

* Understanding the world – The world

Also

* Communication and language – Listening and attention

Equipment and resources

Pictures of farm animals (optional).

Activity

Talk about pets that are often owned by children who live on farms or in the country. You could show the children pictures of animals such as a lamb, goat, piglet or pony. Suggest why some children could own such pets and some could not. Discuss why it may not be practical to keep a pig in a flat.

Extension

Take the children on an outing to visit a farm, or arrange for a 'mobile farm' group to bring some of the smaller and tamer farm animals to visit your setting. Offer children opportunities to stroke and handle some of the animals, but be extremely vigilant about hygiene, ensuring that they wash their hands thoroughly after touching animals and before touching their faces and mouths or eating and drinking. Invite parents and carers to join in with the visits if they would like to and either ask for donations to pay for the activity or use some money that was earned at fundraising events.

Discussion

Talk about the names for baby animals: kid/goat, lamb/sheep, etc, and the names for males and females: billy/nanny, ram/ewe.

Working pets

Learning opportunities
* Understanding that some animals can be pets but also help human beings and the various ways that they can work and help

Links to the Early Learning Goals
* Understanding the world – People and communities, The world

Equipment and resources
An owner/handler of a 'working pet' and his/her animal. (This could be a police officer and dog, a deaf person and hearing dog, a blind person and guide dog, a farmer and sheepdog, a puppy walker and puppy in training or a hospital visitor and petting dog.) Ensure that it is safe for the animal to be handled by the children.

Activity
Invite the owner/handler to meet the group to talk very briefly about the animal and to answer the children's questions. They might like to know what the animal does while it's working, what it likes to do best and how it was trained. Offer children the opportunity to touch or stroke the animal if it is definitely safe for them to do so, but take especial care to reassure any children who are frightened of it and do not expect those who are not keen to go too close.

Extension

Encourage the children to make pictures of the animal and to contribute to a group 'thank you' card. Explain that it is good manners to send these to the owner/handler who kindly came to talk to them.

Discussion

Talk about pets that help us and the jobs they do: police dogs; rescue dogs of all kinds, such as those who search in earthquake-damage zones for people who may be trapped; mountain rescue dogs; hearing and guide dogs who help individual people with specific needs. Research with the children to find out whether only dogs can be trained to work in these ways, or whether any other kind of animal helps people.

Snailarium

Learning opportunities

* Making a study of snails and how to provide a
  suitable habitat and care for them

Links to the Early Learning Goals

* Understanding the world – The world

Equipment and resources

A small collection of a range of snails (different sizes,
colours, types); a clean fish tank (or something similar
with a ventilated lid); garden soil; a patch of garden
lawn turf; a bit of a branch; some medium size stones;
a small box to collect snails in; some suitable snail
food, such as cabbage and lettuce leaves and slices of
pear and banana; non-fiction books on snails.

Activity

Introduce a topic of snails using non-fiction books
and stories, songs, rhymes and drama activities and
encourage the children to discuss the concept of
making a home for snails and what they will need.
Gather the equipment together and prepare the tank
(the new home) with the children's help. When all is
ready, take small groups of children outside (two or
three maximum with two adults) to look for snails.
Each group should only select two or three snails.
Look for suitable foods for the snails to eat and add
these to the tank. Remind the children to wash their
hands thoroughly after handling the equipment and
the snails.

You will need to make sure the turf stays damp.
Place the tank away from direct sunlight or radiators.
After one or two weeks release the snails gently and
carefully into the outdoors again. You could collect
some new ones.

Extension

Look at the trails the snails leave on black paper
and watch how they move either up the side of the
snailarium or on clear plastic. Look at how they eat.

Discussion

Encourage the children to observe the snails closely
and to touch them gently. Ask them what shape
they would call a snail's shell and what it feels like.
Discuss whether all the snails they found are the
same size and colour, or different sizes with different
colours and patterns.

What gerbils eat

Learning opportunities
* Observing gerbils and finding out what they eat

Links to the Early Learning Goals
* Understanding the world – The world

Equipment and resources
Gerbil or photographs/pictures of gerbils; dry gerbil food (available from your pet shop); shallow containers; PVA glue; spreaders; broken-up cereal boxes, white card (not too thin, as it must support fairly weighty collages).

Activity
This is an ideal activity if you have a gerbil as a pet within the setting. If not, you could ask the staff and children and their families if anyone knows someone who owns a gerbil and might be prepared to bring it to visit the children or to lend it to you for a day. Otherwise, show the children pictures or photographs of gerbils. Show the gerbil food to the children and ask them to describe what it looks and feels like. Watch the gerbils eating and notice how their faces look while they are eating.

Invite children to make collages using the dry gerbil food.

Extension

Encourage children to select different items from the mixed gerbil food and sort them into different groups.

Discussion

Talk about what other pets eat and whether rabbits, hamsters or guinea pigs eat the same food as gerbils. Ask children whether they think cats and dogs could eat that type of food and whether they know what all animals drink.

Tropical fish mobiles

Learning opportunities
* Researching the variety of colours and shapes of tropical fish

Links to the Early Learning Goals
* Understanding the world – The world
Also
* Expressive arts and design – Being imaginative

Equipment and resources
Posters or books showing the variety and splendour of tropical fish; A5 sheets of white paper; coloured pens, crayons and pencils; scissors; fish templates (different shapes and sizes); sticky tape; strong thread or thin wool.

Activity
Show the children the posters and books of tropical fish. Discuss the different colours, sizes and shapes. Invite children to colour in a sheet of A5 paper (either or both sides), choosing their own colours and patterns. Then offer them some fish templates and support them in drawing around them to make as many fish as possible. Offer help or support as necessary while they cut out the fish they have drawn.

Extension

Turn one area of the room into a tropical water scene.
Children could help to prepare the backdrop. Stick a
length of thread or wool on to fish and suspend them
from the ceiling. Take the children in small groups on
a visit to the local tropical fish shop/centre.

Discussion

Fish like to swim/stay in their own groups (shoals).
Sometimes the shoals have hundreds of fish in them.

Creepy crawly lotto

Learning opportunities
* Understanding the functions and abilities of common machines that are often used within homes or early years settings
* Developing an awareness of the features of some unusual and exotic pets

Links to the Early Learning Goals
* Understanding the world – Technology
Also
* Understanding the world – The world

Equipment and resources
Coloured pictures of unusual pets (try asking in specialist shops/centres if they have any copies of old magazines or catalogues that they don't need, or use picture books or illustrated encyclopedias); paper; scissors; glue; A5 pieces of card; photocopier, laminator.

Activity
Working with small groups of children at a time, invite them to choose the pictures that they would like to include in a lotto game. Support the children as they cut up and stick the pictures onto A5 sheets of paper, in typical picture lotto style. Make two or more colour photocopies of each sheet and mount them both on the A5 sheets of card. Cut up one sheet of each set of pictures into individual animals. Laminate the game boards and the individual picture cards. Demonstrate how to use the photocopier and the

laminator to make the game and allow children to carry out safe tasks, such as pressing the buttons and collecting the finished sheets, under adult supervision.

Play the lotto game with the children by taking turns to match the cards to the game boards, either taking them from a central pile or scattering them face down and turning them over. Encourage the children to look for distinguishing features, eg different skin colours, shapes, sizes, their different bodies, legs, feet, etc.

Extension

Take the children on a trip to a local pet shop that keeps unusual pets or arrange a visit to the setting by an organization that brings exotic creatures for the children to see and possibly handle. Reassure any children who are worried and only ask them to touch the creatures if they are keen to do so. Invite parents and carers to join in with the visits if they wish to and ask for donations or hold a fundraising event to meet the costs.

Discussion

Encourage children to ask questions and help them to find out more information from books and websites about what foods the animals eat, how they move, where they live and what they do.

I went for a walk one morning

Learning opportunities
* Using imagination to move around in response to an action rhyme
* Thinking of relevant ideas of their own to add to and develop the activity

Links to the Early Learning Goals
* Expressive arts and design – Being imaginative
Also
* Communication and language – Listening and attention

Equipment and resources
Room to move around freely; to be familiar with the structure of the following rhyme:

I went for a walk one morning and what did I see?
(walk around)
I saw a big or small… who was looking at me.
(stand still and look around)
I said 'Good morning'. What do you think he'd say?
(keep standing still)
(Make noise of animal.) You're right! – he did!
And then he (ran/flew) away.
(Say lines, then continue walking, going back to first line)

Activity

Encourage the children to suggest animals and to create a wide variety of appropriate movements, actions and sounds. These could be popular pets (eg a dog), or more unusual ones (eg a bear).

Extension

Ask the children what animals they might see if they went for a real walk. Make a note of their suggestions. Take small groups of children out for a walk. Look for any animals on the way, using the list to mark off any animals the group sees. When you get back indoors, talk about animals with the children and use the list to remind them which animals they saw.

Discussion

Chat with the children about different animals, what noises they make and how they move. Some creatures walk, run or fly, but offer new vocabulary words to help the children to describe others, such as creep, slither, pounce, waddle or squirm.

I can paint a...

Learning opportunities
* Creating a recognizable painting of a pet by closely observing and copying a picture or photograph
* Selecting and mixing paints to create required colours and shades

Links to the Early Learning Goals
* Expressive arts and design – Exploring and using media and materials

Also
* Understanding the world – The world

Equipment and resources
Pots of paint in the primary colours – red, yellow and blue – and black and white; empty pots for colour mixing; photographs of the children's pets; pictures of pets in books and magazines and on posters; paint brushes; large sheets of paper; easels or tables; Blu-tack®; animal templates.

Activity
Use the Blu-tack® to fix each child's photograph or chosen magazine picture to a corner of their easel or table, close to their paper. Encourage children to look very carefully at the picture as they paint their own impression of the animal. This particular activity is intended to develop children's skills of observation and colour matching, so support them in copying as closely as possible and in mixing paints together until the right shade is reached. Younger or less co-ordinated children could even use templates as a

starting point to allow them to achieve the size and outline of their animal. (Offer lots of opportunities for free creative and imaginative painting at other times.)

Extension

Label each painting with the child's name and the name of the pet. Encourage the children to look at and talk about the paintings together and to spot the similarities and differences.

Discussion

Ask children what colours their pets are, which pets are the same colour all over and which have two or more colours or patterns. Talk about the paint colours and remind children of how they made brown or grey or any other colours they needed.

Snail trail

Learning opportunities
* Exploring a new art technique, using paints and wax crayons or candles, to create an original snail trail design

Links to the Early Learning Goals
* Expressive arts and design – Exploring and using media and materials, Being imaginative

Equipment and resources
Plain white thick paper or thin card; white crayons or white household-type candles; paint mixed with lots of water to make a thin wash texture (in any colours); flat brushes (small household brushes are lovely to use for this); snails or pictures of snails and their trails.

Activity
This activity works well with *Snailarium* (page 42). Work with one or two children at a time. Show them pictures of trails made by snails or let them observe an actual snail's trail. Invite them to make their own 'snail trail' pictures. Ask the children to draw lines onto white paper/card with the white crayons or candles (they may need to apply a little pressure). When they brush paint wash over the whole sheet they will reveal their white snail trails!

Extension

Children could be encouraged to follow the trails with their index fingers. This will promote eye–hand coordination and control, and aid concentration. Children could draw a snail on to the paper when the painting is dry.

Discussion

Talk about how fast a snail or slug moves. Ask the children to guess how long it would take a snail to make the trails on their papers.

Sounds like our pets

Learning opportunities
* Exploring expressions and body movements
  through animal role play
* Listening and concentration skills

Links to the Early Learning Goals
* Expressive arts and design – Being imaginative
Also
* Communication and language – Listening and
  attention
* Physical development – Moving and handling

Equipment and resources
No special equipment.

Activity
Ask the children to stand very still to watch and
listen to the adult who is leading the game and then
to make up their own movements and actions. When
the adult makes the sound or the face of a pet animal
(eg the barks of a dog or the nose twitches of a rabbit),
the children may pretend to be that animal. When the
adult stops and stands quietly, the children should
stop too and wait for the next animal.

Extension

Encourage the children to imitate more exotic pets, eg a snake, spider or parrot.

Discussion

Talk with the children about all the different ways that pets move. Some walk or run on four legs, but some hop, jump or fly. Small ones may even have a ball or a wheel to move around in.

Aunty Flo had a...

Learning opportunities
* Developing and improving control and coordination of large and whole body movements
* Using imagination in role play

Links to the Early Learning Goals
* Expressive arts and design – Being imaginative
Also
* Physical development – Moving and handling

Equipment and resources
Space for movement.

Activity
Suggest to the children that they change the words of the song 'Old Macdonald Had A Farm' to be similar to this:

Aunty Flo lived in a bus
E – I – E – I – O
and in that bus she kept a …

Encourage the children to choose pet animals for Aunty Flo and to suggest appropriate actions for each one. Ask them to consider, for example, how a dog walks or runs or how a tortoise moves.

Extension

Encourage the children to suggest appropriate noises as well. Ask the children how large their chosen pet is. If it is large, exaggerate the noises and actions. If it is small, make small actions and very quiet noises.

Discussion

Ask the children to think about the different types of pets that Aunty Flo might have if she lived in different places, such as in the jungle or under the sea. For example, if Aunty Flo lived in a tiny house like a doll's house, what would she have room for? The children will need to think about and name tiny creatures/insects.

Making a snail

Learning opportunities
* Exploring and using craft resources to develop cutting and manipulative skills
* Selecting and using mark making tools
* Designing and making patterns

Links to the Early Learning Goals
* Expressive arts and design – Exploring and using media and materials, Being imaginative
Also
* Understanding the world – The world

Equipment and resources
Snails or pictures of snails; magnifying glass; thin card (A4) ruled into 3 cm strips lengthways; scissors; pens, pencils, crayons and chalks; sticky tape; thin straws.

Activity
Encourage the children to look through the magnifying glass at the colours and patterns on the snails' shells. Demonstrate how to cut along a ruled line to make a thin strip of card and offer help or support to some children as necessary. Invite the children to choose how to colour their snails and to colour both sides of the card strips, using whichever tools they prefer. Demonstrate how to roll up about three-quarters of one end of the strip to form the snail's shell, then help the child(ren) to do the same.

Prepare small bits of tape to fix on the underside

to keep shell shape then offer help and support as necessary while the children do this and fix the shells in place with small pieces of sticky tape. Bend the remaining ends upwards and invite the children to draw on some eyes and stick on two short pieces of straw to be antennae.

Extension

Have a snail race. Tie a piece of strong thread or thin wool to the front underside of each snail. Wrap the other end of each piece of thread or wool around a pencil. Invite children to line their snails up and try to turn the pencils round and round quickly in order to reel in their snails.

Discussion

Ask children whether they think snails can climb or balance on anything and what might be suitable or unsuitable surfaces for them and why. Talk about whether it takes longer for snails to climb up surfaces or to slide down.

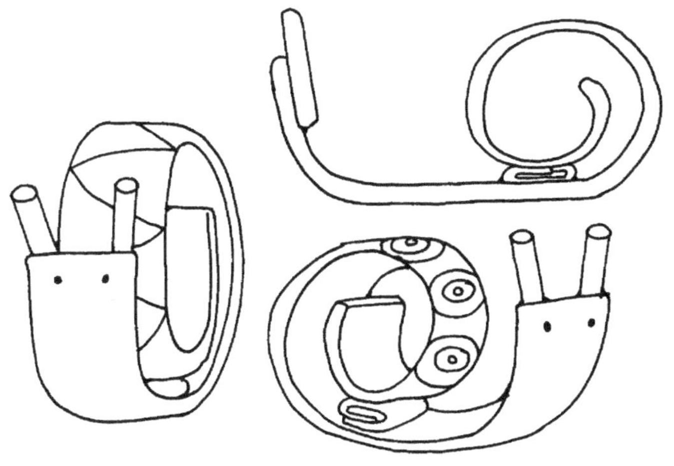